GREEN CRAFTS

Cool Crafts
with
Flowers, Leaves, and Twigs

by Jen Jones

green projects for Resourceful Kids

CAPSTONE PRESS
a capstone imprint

Snap Books are published by Capstone Press,
151 Good Counsel Drive, P.O. Box 669, Mankato, Minnesota 56002.
www.capstonepub.com

Books published by Capstone Press are manufactured with paper
containing at least 10 percent post-consumer waste.

Library of Congress Cataloging-in-Publication Data
Jones, Jen.
  Cool crafts with flowers, leaves, and twigs : green projects for resourceful kids / by Jen Jones.
    p. cm.—(Snap books. Green crafts)
  Summary: "Step-by-step instructions for crafts made from flowers, leaves, and twigs and information about
reusing and recycling"—Provided by publisher.
  Includes bibliographical references and index.
  ISBN 978-1-4296-4766-3 (library binding)
  1. Nature craft—Juvenile literature. 2. Recycling (Waste, etc.)—Juvenile literature. I. Title.

TT157.J645 2011
745.5—dc22

                    2010027901

Editorial Credits
Lori Shores, editor; Gene Bentdahl, designer; Sarah Schuette, photo stylist;
    Marcy Morin, project production; Laura Manthe, production specialist

Photo Credits
All photos by Capstone Studio/Karon Dubke except:
Jen Jones, 32
Shutterstock/Amy Johansson (chain link fence); Ian O'Hanlon (recycling stamp)

Essential content terms are **bold** and are defined at the bottom of the page
where they first appear.

Printed in the United States of America in North Mankato, Minnesota.
092010
005933CGS11

Table of Contents

6

8

10

12

18

26

Introduction

For awesome art supplies, you don't need to go far. Thanks to Mother Nature, many supplies can be found in your own backyard! From flowers to leaves to twigs, a little gathering on your part can go a long way. Using natural items for crafts isn't just inexpensive. It's also a great way to reuse Earth's materials and let them live on for a lot longer. Now that's music to our **eco-friendly** ears!

Reusing flowers, leaves, and twigs also helps cut down on waste. That's a great green move because yard waste takes up a lot of valuable **landfill** space. Instead, create crafts that are chock-full of earthy appeal. Once you dig in, your creativity is sure to bloom and grow.

eco-friendly—marked by or showing concern for the environment

landfill—an area where garbage is stacked and covered with dirt

Go Metric!

It's easy to change measurements to metric! Just use this chart.

To change	into	multiply by
inches	centimeters	2.54
inches	millimeters	25.4
feet	meters	.305
yards	meters	.914

Did You Know?

Composting is another way to cut down on yard waste. Collect leaves, grass clippings, pine needles, and more in a compost bin. By doing so, you'll help feed the Earth and save it too. Composting creates healthy garden soil and keeps yard waste out of landfills. It's a win-win for everyone!

compost—to make a mixture of rotted leaves, vegetables, manure, and other items that can be added to soil to make it richer

Petaled Pretties

Learning how to press flowers is key to creating many cool crafts. Flattening flowers is easy and takes just a few simple steps. Start by collecting some bloomin' beauties. Violets, pansies, and daisies are just a few flowers that are easy to press. You can also press leaves the same way.

Here's what you need:
- scissors
- fresh flowers
- ruler
- thick phone book
- facial tissues
- acid-free paper

1

2

Step 1
Snip the flowers from their stems, leaving about ½ inch of each stem attached.

Step 2
Open a phone book about one-eighth from the back. Place a facial tissue on the page.

Step 3
Arrange flowers on half of the facial tissue, leaving about ½ inch between them. Fold the other half of the tissue over the flowers. Close about another one-eighth of the phone book over the tissue and flowers.

Step 4
Continue placing flowers inside folded tissues in the phone book until all the flowers are arranged.

Step 5
Place something heavy on top of the closed phone book, such as heavy books or another household item.

Step 6
Let the flowers dry for two weeks. If they're still damp, let them dry for another week and check again. When they're completely dry, remove them from inside the tissues and store on acid-free paper.

Tip: Be sure to pick your flowers when they're dry so they are easier to press. Don't pick them when they're still wet with morning dew or the flowers will dry unevenly.

Ray of Light

Light up your life with these classy candleholders. The combo of tissue paper, **decoupage** glue, and pretty flowers creates an unforgettable frosted effect. Light them up, and let all of your hard work shine through.

Here's what you need:

- newspaper
- 1 sheet of tissue paper, any color
- small foam brush
- decoupage glue
- votive candleholder, clear glass
- pressed flowers and/ or leaves (see page 6 for instructions)
- acrylic spray sealer
- battery-operated tea light candle

Tip: You can easily make your own decoupage glue. Just mix a solution of one-half water and one-half white glue in a bowl.

1

2

Step 1
Cover your workspace with newspaper. Tear tissue paper into 1-inch pieces. Set aside.

Step 2
Using a small foam brush, apply a layer of decoupage glue to the outside of a glass votive candleholder.

Step 3
Place pressed flowers onto the candleholder. Apply a thin layer of glue over the flowers.

Step 4
Arrange pieces of tissue paper over the flowers while the glue is still wet. The pieces can overlap or be spaced apart. Be sure that the paper does not reach higher than the top edge of the candleholder.

Step 5
Add another thin layer of decoupage glue. Let dry completely.

Step 6
Take the candleholder outside or to an open space and place it on newspaper. Spray the candleholder with acrylic sealer following the instructions and safety precautions on the spray can.

Step 7 *(not pictured)*
When the sealer is dry, apply a second coat of decoupage glue as you did in step 5. Let dry completely.

Step 8 *(not pictured)*
When the candleholder is completely dry, place a battery-operated tea light candle in the bottom.

decoupage—the art of decorating a surface by pasting on pieces of paper and then covering the whole object with layers of glue

Terrific Twigs

This stylish vase just might steal the show from the flowers. Made using twigs, this nature vase isn't just a nifty decoration. It's extra eco-friendly because you can reuse a glass jar too.

Here's what you need:
- glass jar, clean
- ruler
- wire snips
- twigs, ¼-inch thick
- glue gun and hot glue
- ribbon, ¾-inch wide

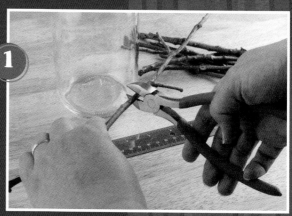

1

2

Step 1
Measure the height of a jar with a ruler. Have an adult use wire snips to cut twigs to 1 inch longer than the jar.

Step 2
Apply a thin line of hot glue to one twig.

Step 3
Press the twig onto the jar. Hold the twig in place for about 15 seconds.

Step 4
Repeat steps 2 and 3 until the jar is covered with twigs. Be sure to place each twig close to the previous one so the jar doesn't show.

Step 5
Tie a ribbon around the middle of the vase.

Step 6
Hot glue the ribbon in place.

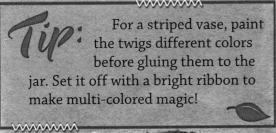

Tip: For a striped vase, paint the twigs different colors before gluing them to the jar. Set it off with a bright ribbon to make multi-colored magic!

Bloom Bites

Many types of flowers don't just smell good. They taste good too! Violets, impatiens, and pansies are **edible** flowers. Make sure you pick flowers from your own garden, though, because flowers grown with chemicals can make you sick. For a special treat, add sugar to flowers and put them on desserts. The fact that this project is eco-friendly is just icing on the cake!

Here's what you need:
- **tray**
- **wax paper**
- **2 tablespoons water**
- **2 tablespoons powdered egg white** (available in baking aisle of grocery store)
- **2 small bowls**
- **fork**
- **fresh edible flowers**, with stem cut to ½ inch
- **small watercolor paint brush, unused**
- **fine strainer**
- **¼ cup sugar**
- **airtight container**

1

2

Step 1
Cover a tray with wax paper and set aside.

Step 2
Combine water and powdered egg white in a small bowl. Beat together with a fork.

Step 3
Hold one flower by the stem. Use a small watercolor brush to paint the water mixture on the petals.

Step 4
Hold the flower above another small bowl. Use a fine strainer to sprinkle sugar over the flower.

Step 5
Set the flower on the tray covered with wax paper.

Step 6 *(not pictured)*
Repeat steps 3 through 5 until you have enough flowers to decorate your special dessert. Let dry overnight.

Step 7 *(not pictured)*
Store flowers in an airtight container until you are ready to use them.

Tip: Do your research before eating any flower. Some flowers, such as the daffodil, iris, and lily of the valley, can make you sick.

edible—safe to eat

Dream On

According to some American Indian traditions, dream catchers trap your dreams in their weblike patterns. The dreams spin around the web, and only good ones make it through. Ward off nasty nightmares with this darling dream catcher. Simply hang it above your bed and get ready for some sweet dreams.

Here's what you need:
- 1 flexible willow twig, about 3 feet long
- thin wire
- scissors
- dental floss
- 1 large bead
- 3 pieces of thin twine, about 6 inches long
- 3 feathers

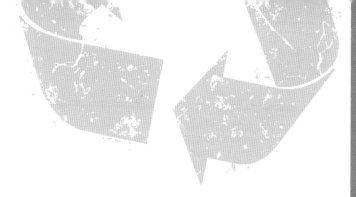

Step 1
Gently bend a twig into a hoop. Fasten the ends together with a small piece of thin wire.

Step 2
Cut a piece of dental floss to be about five times the length of your arm. Knot one end of the floss to the top of the hoop. Snip off the short end of the floss.

Step 3
Make six evenly spaced half-hitch knots around the hoop in a clockwise direction. Keep the floss tight as you work, being careful not to change the shape of the hoop.

Step 4
Make another row of the web by making half-hitch knots in the centers of the open loops of the previous row.

How to make a half-hitch knot:
Loop the dental floss over the twig from the front, or the side facing you, to the back. Pull the end of the floss back to the front through the loop you've just made.

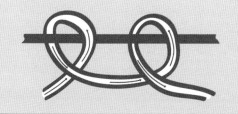

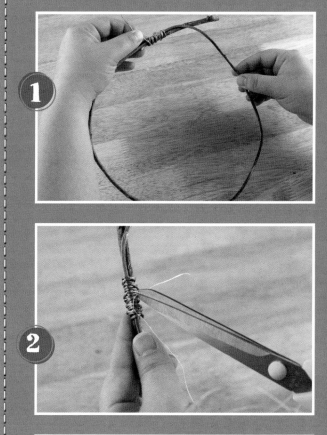

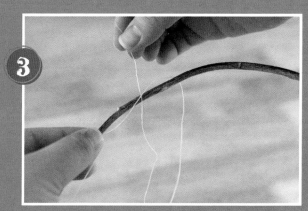

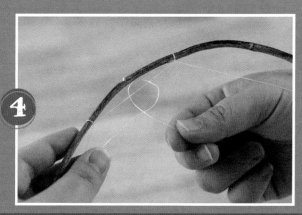

To finish this project, turn to the next page.

Step 5
Continue adding rows to the web until you are left with a small circle in the center of the web.

Step 6
Tie a knot in the floss close to the last half-hitch knot.

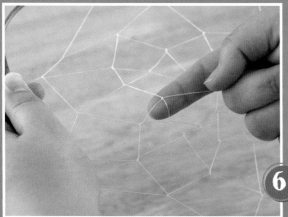

Step 7
Thread the end of the floss through a large bead. Pull the bead close to the knot you made in step 6. Then make another knot in the floss to keep the bead in place. Snip off the end of the floss.

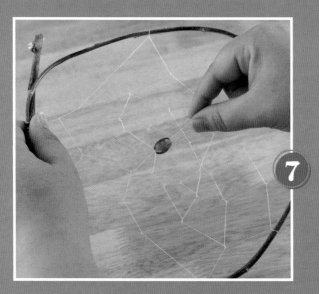

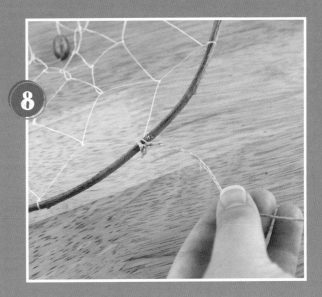

Step 8

Tie a piece of thin twine to the bottom of the dream catcher. Snip off the short end of the twine.

Step 9

Tie the other end of the twine to a feather.

Step 10

Repeat steps 8 and 9 two more times, placing the twine to the left and right of the first piece.

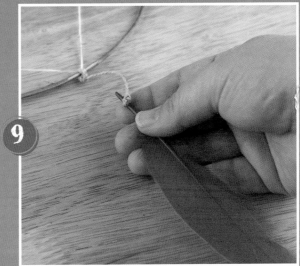

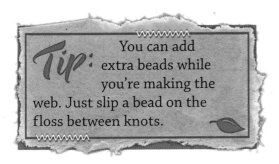

Tip: You can add extra beads while you're making the web. Just slip a bead on the floss between knots.

Custom Coasters

Make any table more exciting with beverages that sit in style. These sweet flower coasters are sure to make you smile every time you pick up your glass.

XXXX

Here's what you need:
- marker
- large soup can
- clear vinyl placemat
- 4 felt squares, 4 inches wide by 4 inches long
- scissors
- tacky glue
- cotton swabs
- pressed flowers and/ or leaves (see page 6 for instructions)
- clear contact paper
- glue gun and hot glue
- thin twine

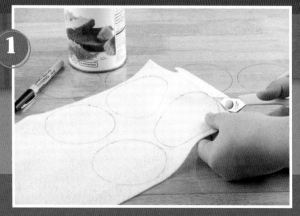

Step 1

Using a marker to trace a large soup can, draw four circles on a vinyl placemat. Then trace the can on each piece of felt. Cut out the circles with scissors.

Step 2

Use tacky glue to attach the felt circles to the undersides of the vinyl circles.

Step 3

Use a cotton swab to apply a small amount of glue to the backsides of the pressed items. Arrange the flowers and leaves on top of the vinyl circles.

Step 4

Trace the soup can four times onto clear contact paper and cut out each circle. Peel the backing away from the circles and press to the coasters.

Step 5

Hot glue twine around the edges of each coaster to make a border.

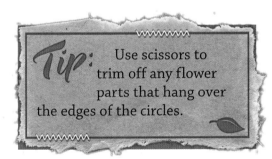

Tip: Use scissors to trim off any flower parts that hang over the edges of the circles.

Sign Language

Ever have a tough time keeping nosy siblings out of your room? Never fear. This sign is sure to mark your territory and spice up your space. Before you begin, decide what you want the sign to say. It might say, "Keep out!" or "Madi's Room." Anything from a welcome sign to a fun phrase is sure to look great.

Here's what you need:
- **wood board, large enough for your chosen words**
- newspaper
- small foam paintbrush
- acrylic paint, any color
- sawtooth picture hanger
- wire snips
- several twigs, ¼-inch thick
- glue gun and hot glue

Step 1

Place a wood board on newspaper. Use a small foam paintbrush to apply a coat of acrylic paint to the front of the board. Let dry.

Step 2

Ask an adult to help you attach a sawtooth picture hanger to the back of the board.

Step 3

Have the adult use wire snips to cut twigs into pieces to make letters.

Step 4

Arrange the twigs on the board to spell out your chosen message.

Step 5

Hot glue each twig piece in place one at a time. Let dry.

Tip: For perfect letters, measure and draw them on paper first. Then use the letter outlines to create your twig letters.

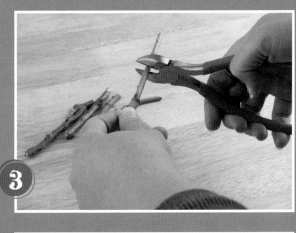

3

4

5

Fall Memories

Forget caterpillars turning into butterflies. This project transforms fall leaves into gorgeous creations! Start by gathering and **preserving** colorful leaves. Then arrange them to show off their beauty. You'll finish with a framed **collage** that will remind you of fall any time of year.

XXXX

Here's what you need:
- **glass baking dish**
- **glycerin**
- **water**
- **fall leaves**
- **small stones**
- **paper towels**
- **2 8-inch x 10-inch**
  pieces of construction
  paper in 2 colors
- **ruler**
- **pencil**
- **scissors**
- **craft glue**
- **cotton swabs**
- **8-inch x 10-inch frame**

XXXX

Step 1
In a glass baking dish, mix ¼ cup glycerin and ½ cup water.

Step 2
Place leaves in a single layer in the glycerin and water mixture. Weigh down the leaves with small stones to keep them underwater.

Step 3 *(not pictured)*
Set the baking dish somewhere it won't be disturbed. Let the leaves sit in the mixture for four days.

Step 4
Remove leaves from glycerin and dry with paper towels.

preserve—to protect something so that it stays in its original condition

collage—a variety of pictures or other materials arranged and glued onto a piece of paper

To finish this project, turn to the next page.

Step 5
Select a sheet of construction paper for the border. Then draw a box that measures 1½ inches in from the edge of the paper on all sides.

Step 6
Cut out the box to create the border. Glue the border onto the background paper.

Step 7
Use a cotton swab to apply glue to the back of a leaf.

XXXX

XXXX

Step 8
Press leaf down onto the background paper.

Step 9 *(not pictured)*
Repeat steps 7 and 8 with other leaves to complete the collage. The leaves can be placed inside the border or overlap it. Let dry completely.

Step 10
Remove the back of an 8- by 10-inch frame and place collage in frame. Replace the back of the frame.

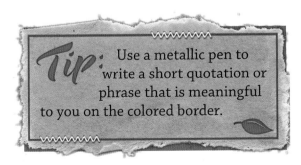

Tip: Use a metallic pen to write a short quotation or phrase that is meaningful to you on the colored border.

Forest Frame

Branch out with an entirely different kind of photo frame! This forest-inspired frame adds a touch of woodsy wonder to any wall. Once you collect your twiggy tools, you'll have a blast framing the day away.

Here's what you need:
- wire snips
- 12 twigs, about ¼-inch thick
- ruler
- craft glue
- 4-inch by 6-inch photo
- cardboard, cut to 6 inches wide by 8 inches long
- glue gun and hot glue
- 4 acorns (optional)
- ¼-inch wide ribbon, 6 inches long

1

2

Step 1
Have an adult use wire snips to cut six twigs to 9 inches long. Have the adult cut another six twigs to 7 inches long.

Step 2
Use craft glue to attach a photo to the center of the cardboard.

Step 3
Lay the twigs around the photo to see how they will fit. The longer twigs will be glued across the top and bottom. The shorter twigs will be glued along the sides.

Step 4
Once you have a layout you like, hot glue the twigs in place one at a time. Be sure to cover all the cardboard.

Step 5 *(optional)*
For a decorative touch, hot glue an acorn to each corner of the frame.

Step 6
Hot glue one end of a ribbon to the backside of the frame at the top left corner. Hot glue the other end to the backside at the top right corner to make a loop for hanging.

Tip: For more pizzazz, use glitter paint to spruce up the twigs before making the frame.

Green Crafting Facts

🐞 Don't just hug a tree, plant one! Trees do lots of good for the **environment**. They help reduce pollution by absorbing carbon dioxide and cut down on global warming. Plus, we couldn't make such cool crafts without 'em!

🐞 Go, go, H_2O! Everyone runs water to warm it up before a shower. Put a bucket under the tub faucet to collect that wasted water. After your shower, use that water to keep your plants and flowers bloomin' fresh.

🐞 Don't let lawn waste go to waste. Yard waste takes up lots of landfill space—almost 20 percent of total yearly waste. Encourage your family to use grass clippings for **mulch**. Save colorful leaves for your next craft. Then bring what you can't use to your local compost site.

environment—the natural world of the land, water, and air

mulch—a layer of sawdust, paper, or dead plants spread on soil to condition it

🐞 Flowers are beautiful, but there can be a not-so-pretty side to the floral business. Chemicals are often used for growing flowers. **Organic** flower businesses are popping up right and left. Next time you need to order flowers, look for shops that offer eco-friendly bouquets.

organic—using only natural products and no chemicals

Glossary

collage (kuh-LAHZH)—a variety of pictures or other materials arranged and glued onto a piece of paper

compost (KOM-pohst)—to make a mixture of rotted leaves, vegetables, manure, and other items that can be added to soil to make it richer

decoupage (day-koo-PAHZH)—the art of decorating a surface by pasting on pieces of paper and then covering the whole object with layers of glue

eco-friendly (EE-koh-frend-lee)—inflicting minimal or no harm to the environment; eco-friendly is short for ecologically friendly

edible (ED-uh-buhl)—able to be eaten

environment (in-VY-ruhn-muhnt)—the natural world of the land, water, and air

global warming (GLOH-buhl WOR-ming)—the gradual temperature rise of Earth's atmosphere

landfill (LAND-fill)—an area where garbage is stacked and covered with dirt

mulch (MUHLCH)—a layer of sawdust, paper, or dead plants spread on soil to condition it

organic (or-GAN-ik)—using only natural products and no chemicals

preserve (pri-ZURV)—to protect something so that it stays in its original condition

Read More

Anton, Carrie. *Earth Smart Crafts: Transform Toss-away Items into Fun Accessories, Gifts, Room Décor, and More!* Middleton, Wis.: American Girl, 2009.

Coley, Mary McIntyre. *Environmentalism: How You Can Make a Difference.* Take Action. Mankato, Minn.: Capstone Press, 2009.

Sirrine, Carol. *Cool Crafts with Old Wrappers, Cans, and Bottles: Green Projects for Resourceful Kids.* Green Crafts. Mankato, Minn.: Capstone Press, 2010.

RECYCLE

Internet Sites

FactHound offers a safe, fun way to find Internet sites related to this book. All of the sites on FactHound have been researched by our staff.

Here's all you do:

Visit *www.facthound.com*

Type in this code: **9781429647663**

Index

About the Author

A Midwesterner-turned-California girl, Jen Jones loves to be in nature and is proud to be part of any project that makes our world a greener place! Jen is a Los Angeles-based writer who has authored more than 35 books for Capstone Press. Her stories have been published in magazines such as *American Cheerleader*, *Dance Spirit*, *Ohio Today*, and *Pilates Style*. She has also written for E! Online, MSN, and PBS Kids, as well as being a Web site producer for major talk shows such as *The Jenny Jones Show*, *The Sharon Osbourne Show*, and *The Larry Elder Show*. Jen is a member of the Society of Children's Book Writers and Illustrators.